Tiffany **MacQu**

Discovering the
Personality
of **Punctuation**

Turning the
Ho Hums
into **Tee Hees**

Kendall Hunt
publishing company

Cover image © Shutterstock.com

Kendall Hunt
p u b l i s h i n g   c o m p a n y
www.kendallhunt.com
Send all inquiries to:
4050 Westmark Drive
Dubuque, IA 52004-1840

Printed in the United States of America

DEDICATION

This book is dedicated to Brian,
Mikayla (fellow grammar nerd), and Noah.

Special thanks to my dear friend, Kathy Atwell,
who always makes time to "red pen" me. I appreciate you!

Contents

PART ONE: Discovering the Personality of Punctuation 1

PART TWO: Grammar 19

PART THREE: Punctuation 41

Discovering the Personality of Punctuation

part 1

INTRODUCTION

Do you choose to play it safe when writing by employing primarily commas and periods? Does the mere thought of using a dash or semicolon cause beads of perspiration on your brow? Discover the personality of punctuation and insert parentheses, colons, and other types of punctuation into your writing with confidence.

People understand that words have power, but there is also great power in punctuation that cannot be overlooked; just ask Grandma:

> *Let's eat Grandma!*

Look at the difference a comma makes:

> *Let's eat, Grandma!*

She goes from entrée to invited guest simply with the insertion of a comma.

You need not convince her that punctuation is powerful.

Here's another one:

A woman without her man is nothing.

Now ladies, relax. The lesson doesn't end there.

Now, without amending the words or the structure of the sentence, look at the difference punctuation can make:

A woman: without her, man is nothing.

(Can I get an "amen," ladies?)

Again, there is power in punctuation, and it is about time to start using it... confidently.

Now, you have probably studied the different marks of punctuation in grade school, but I bet you never studied the *personality behind the punctuation.* (Say what?)

Imagine a classroom. Each student enters the classroom with a common purpose: learn and practice as much as he or she can in order to _____ (insert purpose). Similarly, the dash, comma, and parentheses share a common function—to offset nonessential information or interrupters. So, how do they differ?

Each mark of punctuation has a different personality!

COMMA

The comma has many uses; it is almost like the Sybil of punctuation (multiple personalities).

Use

For the purpose of this discussion, let me remind you of two of its uses:

1. **Interrupting words and expressions**

   Example: The Pennsylvania State University, for example, has twenty-four campuses scattered across the Commonwealth.

2. **Nonessential clause (a clause that can be omitted without changing the sentence's basic meaning)**

   Example: Phyllis, armed with a hot meal and a basket of books and snacks, greeted her sister-in-law with a hug and a smile.

Personality

© Andrey Makurin/Shutterstock.com

Consider the comma to be the **dependable, sensible student**. In the classroom in your mind, the comma is that student who never missed class and is always prepared properly for class. You know that whenever you need help in class, this student will always assist. He or she becomes your go-to student for the class. Similarly, the comma positions itself well as your **go-to** mark of punctuation. It is always available to help you out when you have a nonessential clause or interrupting words or sentences. Just remember to offset both sides of the clause or interrupter with commas.

Note: Practice exercises for commas can be found in Part Two.

DASH

Next, you have the dash. (Note: In typing, a dash is shown by two hyphens—like this—usually with no space before, after, or between.)

Use

1. **Indicate sudden interruptions (usually in speech)**

   Example: It has been three weeks—no, maybe only ten days—since I have consumed a Diet Pepsi.

2. **Provide emphasis**

   Example: Mikayla—ever the drama queen—sulked away with sunken shoulders when she learned that her parents had suspended her data plan for her cell phone.

3. **Introduce summary statements after a series**

   Example: Mopping the stairs, cleaning the bathroom, making your bed, dusting the TV room—all must be completed before noon every Saturday.

Personality

Dashes are essentially the **"class clown"** of punctuation. They function pretty much by shouting, "Hey, look at me!" Yeah, the dash is *that* student. Continuing with the classroom analogy, the class clown frequently interrupts the teacher or professor with comments to attract desired attention to oneself. The dash showboats in a similar fashion. It interrupts the flow of the sentence in order to emphasize the information contained between the dashes. If you want information emphasized, you definitely want to offset it with dashes.

PRACTICE EXERCISE 1.1

Directions: Add a dash where needed.

1. Because I felt ill during my visit with Brian at State College, he drove me in my car the three hours to my house and took the bus a six-hour ride back to campus.

2. "I haven't caught a single" Jason lamented, just as his bobber plunged deep beneath the water.

3. Most of her general education requirements, two major requirements, three option requirements all were completed by the start of Hannah's first year of college, thanks to her college-in-high school program.

4. Every Easter, Tiffany's father best dad ever bought her a corsage, an Easter outfit, and a chocolate egg.

5. Screams erupted from Mikayla's bedroom as birds two of them flew down her chimney and swooped her head.

PARENTHESES

Then you have parentheses.

Use

Parentheses are used to enclose the following:

1. **Loosely related comments or explanations**

   Example: I frequent Subway (which is hands down my favorite fast food restaurant) so often that when I step through the door, the woman at the counter asks, "Your regular?"

2. **Figures that number items in a series**

   Example: Taryn, please do not attempt to drive another of my golf balls over the pond because (1) you have never successfully navigated a ball over this particular pond, (2) four golfers wait behind us to tee off, and (3) this would be your fifth failed attempt at this hole today.

3. **References in documentation**

   Example: In the introduction of Jenny Baranick's book, *Missed Periods and Other Grammar Scares*, she stressed the importance of good writing: "Oftentimes, people meet our writing before they meet us; our writing *is* our first impression" (vii).

4. **Dates of birth, death, and publication**

   Example: Marlene Smith (1948–2011) modeled incredible faith, especially during her battle with cancer.

Personality

Parentheses are the **side whisperers** that sit in the back of the classroom. You know them. (Perhaps you *are* one of them.) The professor lectures, and the student in the back of the room whispers some loosely related comment to the students nearby. The professor stops. "I'm sorry?" The student mumbles, "Nothing," while the handful of students around him or her giggle. In the punctuation world, parentheses feel like they have to provide some loosely related comment, but unlike the dash, they do not want all of the attention. If you wish to share but not showboat (or de-emphasize) information, enclose the words in parentheses.

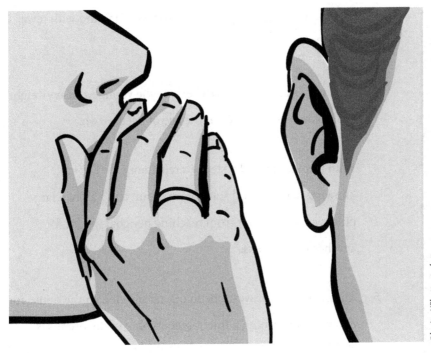

©lavitrei/Shutterstock.com

PRACTICE EXERCISE 1.2

Directions: Add parentheses where needed.

1. Natalia though competitive on the soccer field quickly becomes flustered during the intensity of the game *Anomia*.

2. Athena draws upon Patricia T. O'Conner's words from her book *Words Fail Me* when encouraging her students to replace weak verbs with strong verbs: "An active verb has more energy, more buzz; it gets to the point sooner and with fewer words" 59.

3. Muhammad Ali 1942-2016 became the youngest heavyweight champion boxer in 1964 at the age of twenty-two.

4. With trepidation Kelly stepped reluctantly on the scale knowing her weekend splurge ice cream and half of a large pizza would keep her from reaching her goal weight for another three weeks.

5. Timmy not the bravest one in our family cleared the house for entry by performing a thirty-second scan of the premises.

So you can see that while in theory the comma, dash, and parentheses all have a common purpose, their personality separates them a great deal, so much that it just wouldn't feel right to always settle by using a comma. Why, that's just like settling for a period to end all of your sentences, which brings me to the next two marks of punctuation to include in your writing tool belt: the colon and semicolon.

COLON

The colon is a remarkable tool to cut the number of unnecessary words in a sentence. I often tell my students that a colon is a "party waiting to happen." I assure you that once you understand how to properly use the colon, there will be no turning back.

Use

1. **After a formal introduction of a quotation**

     Example: I offer the same advice every semester to each of my students: "Start strong; Stay strong; End strong."

2. **After a formal introduction of a series of items**

     Example: Each semester, students enrolled in an English Composition course benefit from a review of these common errors: fragments, comma splices, pronoun antecedent agreement, and comma use.

3. **After a formal introduction of an appositive (word, phrase, or clause used as a noun and placed beside another word to explain, identify, or rename it); think of the colon substituting for words such as *namely* and *that is*.**

     Example: My husband, ever the avid archer, froze in wonderment at what stood majestically before him: the twelve-point beauty captured previously only on his game cam.

4. **Between two independent clauses when one explains the other**

   Example: My heart is full: my son fed the dogs *without* being asked or reminded.

5. **After the salutation of a formal letter**

   Dear Mrs. Juanita Kendall:

Note: Do not use a colon after a linking verb or after a preposition.

Personality

In her book *Woe is I,* Patricia T. O'Connor suggests that we think of the colon as **"punctuation's master of ceremonies,"** since it is a more formal mark of punctuation. As a visual learner, I envision the colon standing at the podium dressed in a tux introducing the next act. The curtains part as the hushed audience waits with eager anticipation for what follows. Can you feel the excitement and tension before the curtains open? The colon builds anticipation for what follows. The pause is brief, but palpable.

PRACTICE EXERCISE 1.3

Directions: Add a colon where needed.

1. When trying to make wise food choices, I strive to remember this saying "Nothing tastes as good as thin feels."

2. Taryn packed an abundance of snacks for our trip potato chips, cheese curls, candy, pretzels, and chocolate.

3. Emily employed her nursing skills during her missions trip this spring, but she especially beamed when sharing her greatest experience delivering a baby.

4. After receiving his driver's license, Luke frequently set out for one of his two favorite destinations Dairy Queen or Handel's.

5. Tammi planned lots of fundraisers for her youth group teens interested in attending this year's International Youth Conference bake sales, dinners, breakfasts, yard sales, pepperoni sales, candy sales, and hoagie sales.

SEMICOLON

The semicolon has a different focus altogether.

Use

1. **Between two complete sentences to show a relationship between the two sentences**

   Example: Mikayla is a natural hostess; she takes after her Aunt T. and Uncle Ken I'm told.

2. **To separate complete sentences that are long and complex or have internal punctuation**

   Example: I completed my first Dirty Dash, one of my bucket list items, in August; and just today, my best friend, who in high school could not run farther than fifty yards, completed a 50k trail run.

3. **In a series between items that have internal punctuation**

   Example: I rode a go-cart down Mt. Bromley in Manchester Center, Vermont; hiked the trails in scenic Jackson Hole, Wyoming; and navigated up the perilous heights of Mount Washington in North Conway, New Hampshire.

Personality

Consider the semicolon the **counselor** of punctuation. It is the mark of punctuation whose main goal is to provide clarity. It often brings two complete sentences together and shows a relationship between the two sentences. It steps in to assist the comma in separating items in a series when the comma's hands are already full trying to carry out other necessary tasks within the sentence. It also assists the comma when joining two complete sentences together with a coordinating conjunction (FANBOYS: *for, and, nor, but, or, yet, so*) when, again, the comma is totally occupied with other responsibilities in the sentences. Remember your goal as a writer is to write with as little reader interference as possible. Above all, you want to be understood (Don't we all?); the semicolon can help.

I just want to be understood.

©Cartoonresource/Shutterstock.com

PRACTICE EXERCISE 1.4

Directions: Add a semicolon where needed.

1. Ralph rejoiced when he and Lori finally reached the end of their canoeing expedition the first thing he did was kiss the ground and say, "Thank you, Lord."

2. Amy and John David skillfully navigated the rapids they even paddled up the river to experience them a second time.

3. Phyllis enjoyed her retirement by spending a week in Florida with Beth, Perry, and Tim four days in Houston, Texas with Gordon, Judy, and Tiffany and three days in Bethesda, Maryland with Taryn and Tiffany.

4. Ron retired from his job in Arizona and moved back to Pennsylvania however, he continues to work two days a week.

5. Upon my return from the restroom, I struggled to find my seat again in the darkened movie theater it was Marlene's laugh, however, that directed me to the correct location.

BRACKETS

Are you part of the population who believes that brackets and parentheses can be used interchangeably? Perhaps brackets are the nerdy cousin of the parentheses, you know, a little awkward and square? Um…no!

Use

1. **Insert any editorial comments or amend any part of quoted material**

    Example: "That is hilarious [no visible smile, no laughter heard]," Karen said as she prodded me to continue my story.

2. **Inform the reader that the original quoted material contained an error**

    Example: In kindergarten my son said, "technogoly [sic] is my favorite subject." I loved his mispronunciation.

3. **Provide directions**

    Example: [To be continued.] or [Please turn the page.]

Personality

The brackets are the bossy older siblings of the other marks of punctuation. No, really, tell me the bracket's functions do not ring a bell:

©eladora/Shutterstock.com

- They often insert comments or change some things when you are telling a story.
- They are quick to throw you under the bus by pointing blame.
- They tell you what to do.

I don't know about you, but that eerily resembles the uses listed above, if you ask me. (The truth hurts, huh?)

PRACTICE EXERCISE 1.5

Directions: Add brackets or parentheses where needed.

1. She purchased his Christmas gift though she can't remember where she hid it back in September.

2. "I can't wait to go on vacation!" Noah shouted. "Deep Creek, Maryland is my favorite place to be."

3. Penelope shrugged and dismissed the gesture, "It don't sic matter anyway."

4. "I can't wait for it J.K. Rowling's newest book to come out this year," Kristin relayed to her campers at the Harry Potter camp.

5. For their 50th anniversary, the couple rode around the neighborhood on a golf cart with a sign that read *Just Married again.*

CONCLUSION

So, the comma is the dependable student; the dash, the class clown; parentheses, the side whisperer; the colon, the master of ceremonies; the semicolon, the counselor; and brackets, the bossy older siblings.

It is my hope that you will never view punctuation marks in the same way. They are not simply things to use to end a sentence or marks to tell the reader when to take a breath (in fact, that is not even a legitimate comma rule, by the way). Each mark has a unique purpose and personality. Experiment. Have fun. Kick it up a little; there is power in punctuation!

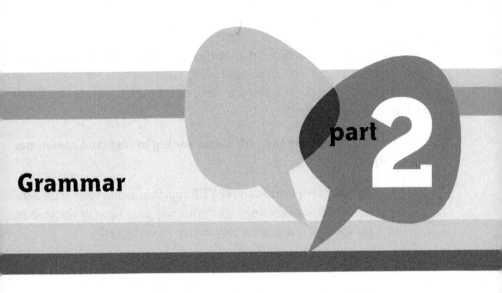

part 2

Grammar

FRAGMENTS

Fragments are basically sentence wannabes. They try really hard to masquerade as sentences, but they simply miss the mark.

Here's why. **All sentences require three elements: a subject, a verb, and a complete thought.** Merely checking off a subject and a verb does NOT guarantee a complete sentence. Look at this example:

Fragment: Though I laughed loudly.

I is the subject, *laughed* is the verb, but it is not a complete thought. If I walked up to you and said, *"Though I laughed loudly"* and walked away, you would probably think *Wait, what?* It doesn't make sense. It was a piece of a sentence punctuated as if it was a complete sentence.

1. **Be on the alert for words that sound the fragment siren.**

After	Although	As	Before	As if	As long as
As soon as	As though	Because	Especially	Even though	For example
If	In order to	Since	So that	Such as	Unless
Until	When	Whenever	Where	Wherever	While
Who	Whom	Whose	Which	Where	

Each time you see a sentence that begins with one of these words, signal your brain to sound the siren: Red alert! Red alert! What follows may be a fragment. Check for a subject, verb, and complete thought BEFORE adding the end punctuation.

2. **Don't be fooled by the verb forms ending in *-ing* (and sometimes *-ed*).**

   - The *-ing* verb forms can **NEVER** function as the verb of the sentence. Most often *-ing* verb forms rely on a form of the verb *be* (*is, was, were, am, been, are*) to step in as the verb.

     Fragment: The chef sharpening his knives before dinner.

     Sentence: The chef *was* sharpening his knives before dinner.

   - The *-ed* verbs are a bit trickier.

     Sometimes they CAN function as the verb.

     Sentence: The player rebounded the ball.

     Sometimes they CANNOT function as the verb.

     Fragment: Daunted by the task before them.

3. **Question the five Ws (*who, whom, where, which, whose*). If the words are not asking a question, likely you have a fragment.**

   Fragment: The cookies, whose smell roused me from my slumber.

   Sentence: Whose cookies are those?

Fragment Fix-its:

1. **Add what's missing**

   Missing Subject: Am looking forward to tomorrow's race.

   Sentence: I am looking forward to tomorrow's race.

   Missing Verb: The girl sitting beside me.

   Sentence: The girl sitting beside me stared intently at the screen.

2. **Join the fragment to the sentence either before or after it.**

   Fragment: Mistakenly believing it was a caterpillar. Kari left the stick on the chair cushion.

   Sentence: Mistakenly believing it was a caterpillar, Kari left the stick on the chair cushion. (Connecting the dependent clause with the independent clause forms a complex sentence.)

PRACTICE EXERCISE 2.1

Directions: Write C beside complete sentences and F beside fragments.

1. My friend, who vowed to never drink Tequila again.

2. Ready when you are.

3. Please hurry!

4. Miranda loving her new job.

5. Kaitlyn squealed with delight at the sight of the pot belly pig.

COMMA SPLICE AND FUSED SENTENCE

The next two types of sentence errors are very similar. The only difference is that the comma splice has a comma separating two complete sentences, and the fused sentence contains no punctuation separating the two.

Comma splice: two complete sentences joined together incorrectly with only a comma

Complete sentence

Example: The toddler looked defiantly into her mother's eyes,

Complete sentence

she threw pieces of pancake over the side of her highchair. (two sentences separated only with a comma)

Fused sentence: two complete sentences joined together incorrectly with no punctuation separating them

Complete sentence

Example: The toddler looked defiantly into her mother's eyes

Complete sentence

she threw pieces of pancake over the side of her highchair. (two sentences separated with no internal punctuation)

If you struggle remembering which is which, think of the name. A **comma splice** uses a **comma to splice** or connect two sentences together. A **fused sentence** uses **no internal punctuation to fuse** together two complete sentences.

Just a reminder that both comma splices and fused sentences are **sentence errors**. They need to be corrected.

Comma Splice and Fused Sentence Fix-its:

1. **Use a period.** I do challenge you to sometimes step outside your comfort zone. Don't always rely on the basic period to get the job done.

   Example: The toddler looked defiantly into her mother's eyes. She threw pieces of pancake over the side of her highchair.

2. **Use one of the seven coordinating conjunctions (FANBOYS:** *For, And, Nor, But, Or, Yet, So*)

   • The comma always goes *before* the coordinating conjunction.

   Example: The toddler looked defiantly into her mother's eyes, **and** she threw pieces of pancake over the side of her highchair.

   • Do not add an additional comma if the error was a comma splice.

   • Only use a comma before a conjunction if both clauses are independent clauses, meaning they both can stand alone as a complete sentence. *Hint:* If both verbs share the same subject, they are not two independent clauses.

   Example of no comma necessary: The toddler looked defiantly into her mother's eyes and threw pieces of pancake over the side of her highchair.

   (Both verbs share the same subject, toddler)

3. **Separate both clauses with a semicolon**

   Example: The toddler looked defiantly into her mother's eyes; she threw pieces of pancake over the side of her highchair.

Before employing a semicolon, think of a stop sign. When you come to a stop sign while driving, you are legally bound to stop. You look to the left and see there are no cars coming. You look to the right and see there are no cars coming. (Always look back to the left. Those cars can seemingly come out of nowhere!) When you determine you can do so safely, you proceed.

Similarly, use that same technique before applying a semicolon. Look to the left and see that the clause is a complete sentence. Look to the right and see that the clause is a complete sentence. (I assure you that there is no need to take a second glance to the left. Sentences usually remain still.) At that point, you can determine that it is safe to use a semicolon.

Be on alert for the following words that may sound the comma splice siren.

Comma Splice Warning Words

As a result	Consequently	Finally	For example
Furthermore	Hence	However	In addition
Moreover	Nevertheless	Next	On the contrary
Similarly	Then	Therefore	Thus

Remember that there must be a complete sentence on both sides of the comma splice warning word for you to correctly add a semicolon. If there is, place a **semicolon before** the warning word and a **comma after** the warning word.

4. **Turn one complete sentence into a dependent clause (fragment) by adding one of the fragment warning words to the beginning of the clause.**

Dependent clause (fragment)

Example: **As** the toddler looked defiantly into her mother's eyes,

she threw pieces of pancake over the side of her highchair.

Independent clause (sentence)

PRACTICE EXERCISE 2.2

Directions: Write CS beside comma splices, FUS beside fused sentences, and C beside complete sentences.

1. Smitten at the first sight of him, Jenny coaxed the kitten from the bushes.

2. Mr. Gray tried to teach Jennifer's friend how to ski, despite his best effort, however, she still plowed head first into the tree.

3. Marissa eagerly shares with anyone who will listen her life has been changed forever!

4. Ethan desired to follow in his father's footsteps, consequently, he works as a welder and volunteers as a firefighter.

5. Chocolate chip cookies beckon Katrina from across the room she must answer their call.

PRONOUN–ANTECEDENT AGREEMENT

An **antecedent** is the word to which the pronoun refers in a sentence.

> Antecedent   pronoun
>
> *Example:* Tammy guided her team through the dusty trails of South Mountain.
>
> (*Her* is the pronoun referring to Tammy; therefore, Tammy is the **antecedent.**)

You need to make sure that the pronoun and antecedent agree in **gender** and **number.** (If the antecedent is singular, then the pronoun needs to be singular. If the antecedent is plural, then the pronoun needs to be plural.)

1. **Indefinite pronouns that end in *-one, -body,* or *-thing* are always singular.**

anyone	no one	someone	everyone
anybody	nobody	somebody	everybody
anything	nothing	something	everything

   > sing. antecedent   sing. pronoun
   >
   > *Example:* Everyone has the right to his or her own opinion.

2. **The following list of indefinite pronouns are always plural:**

both	few	fewer	many
others	several	they	

   > two antecedents
   >
   > *Example:* I can't decide which ice cream to have: turtle or chocolate almond. Both are my favorite.
   >
   > plural pronoun

3. **The following list of indefinite pronouns can be either singular or plural, depending on the context.**

all	any	more	most
none	some	such	

singular

Example: All is well.

plural

All have checked into the hotel already.

4. **Compound antecedents (two or more) joined by *and* are plural.**

   Example: Minecraft and Terraria have their own loyal fan base. (*Their* refers to both *Minecraft* and *Terraria*.)

5. **Compound antecedents (two or more) joined by *or, nor, either... or, neither...nor, not...but,* or *not only...but also* must agree in number with the closer antecedent.**

   singular   singular

   Example: Neither the stars nor the moon could cast its light bright enough to aid the weary traveler.

   plural   plural

   Example: Neither the moon nor the stars could cast their light bright enough to aid the weary traveler.

   If the gender of the antecedent is masculine, use a masculine pronoun; If the antecedent is feminine, use a feminine pronoun.

   feminine antecedent   feminine pronoun

   Example: Julie presented her daughter with her high school diploma at graduation on Friday.

If the gender of the antecedent is unknown, you can:

1. **Include both *his and her* to include either gender**

   Example: Any student who has a signed note from his or her parent can report to the office.

2. **Make both the pronoun and the antecedent plural**

   Example: Students who have a signed note from their parent can report to the office.

3. **Rewrite the sentence to eliminate the pronoun.**

   Example: Students with a signed note from a parent can report to the office.

PRACTICE EXERCISE 2.3

Directions: Correct the sentences to ensure that pronouns are clear and that they agree with their antecedents. Write C beside any correct sentence.

1. Please have the student sign their name and return the form to this office.

2. Lorraine intentionally pitched the softball at the umpire while Kelly (the catcher) moved out of the way. Both were ejected from the game for displaying poor sportsmanship.

3. Neither the presenter nor her colleagues knew how to navigate to her venue when encountering the orange detour signs..

4. Neither the twins nor their older sister were brave enough to sleep in her own bed during the storm.

5. Jessica and her brothers huddled together on the floor of her parent's bedroom.

PRONOUN CASE

It can be so confusing to know whether to use *I* or *me* or *who* or *whom*. Some folks mistakenly go by *sound*, which, more often than not, will be incorrect. They use pronouns such as *I* or *myself*, thinking it makes them sound more academic when the correct pronoun may be *me*.

me
↙

Example: Let's keep this situation between you and I, shall we?

How many times have you heard something similar? If you simply rely on *sound* and do not learn the rules of pronoun case, you may become THAT guy! (Trust me; don't become THAT guy!)

Most of us do not struggle with possessive pronouns (listed below); it is the subjective and objective ones that are tricky.

Subjective Case:	Objective Case:	Possessive Case:
You	You	Your
I	Me	Mine
He	Him	His
She	Her	Hers
It	It	Its
They	Them	Theirs
We	Us	Ours
Who	Whom	Whose

1. **The easiest way to determine which case (objective or subjective) is correct is to remember that if the pronoun is the *subject* of the sentence, use *subjective case*.**

    subject
    ↘ →

    Example: My mother and I visited the Holocaust Museum in Houston, Texas. (Use *subjective* case.)

2. If the pronoun is *not the subject* of the sentence (and is not possessive), use *objective* case. The objective case is used when the pronoun is either the object of the verb or the object of a preposition.

    verb   object

    Example: The smeared chocolate on their faces betrayed them. (The subject is chocolate; therefore, use **objective** case for the pronoun. *Them* is the **object of the verb** *betrayed.*)

3. *Myself* is what's called a *reflexive* pronoun. Please be sure that its antecedent (word to which the pronoun refers) goes *before* it in the sentence.

    antecedent   pronoun

    Example: Mikayla proudly displayed the cake she had made herself for Brady's birthday.

4. The antecedent must also be clear. Using pronouns such as *it, this, that,* and *which* sometimes causes confusion for the reader. Imagine if I walked into the room soaking wet, holding cold coffee and graded tests, and I said, "This is terrible!" To what do you think I would be referring? Rainy weather? Cold coffee? Poor test scores? You could only guess! Don't make the reader guess—make it clear.

Tips

- If the pronoun follows a preposition, then it is **objective.**
- If the pronoun follows a linking verb (such as forms of the verb *be: is, am, was, were*), then it is **subjective.**
- If the pronoun follows words such as *than* or *as,* then it is **subjective.**

PRACTICE EXERCISE 2.4

Directions: Choose the correct word choice in each of the following sentences.

1. Devin, Jessica, Marissa, Natalia, and I/myself played board games the day of graduation.

2. Beth and Phyl collaborated on an anniversary card for Brian and I/me.

3. Yes, this is she/her speaking.

4. We did not know who/whom was to blame.

5. Liz eagerly devoured the book since it was she/her who had suggested it as the group's next study.

PARALLELISM

When you compare two or more things, make sure to use the same grammatical structure for both. Be sure to pair nouns with nouns, verbs with verbs, prepositional phrases with prepositional phrases, infinitive phrases with infinitive phrases, etc.

1. **Match nouns with nouns**

   Example: Ranee packed her vehicle with all the essentials for their beach vacation: sunscreen, towels, food, sheets, games, clothes, and toiletries.

   all nouns

2. **Match verbs with verbs**

   Example: The Leslie family walked the beach, rented paddleboards, and strolled the Boardwalk.

   all verb phrases

3. **Match prepositional phrases with prepositional phrases**

   All prepositional phrases

   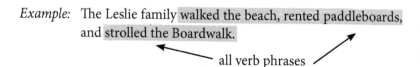

   Example: Jarod sprinted out of bed, down the sidewalk, and onto the bus just as the bus driver arrived at the corner of Park Place and Manhattan Street.

Note: If the same preposition is used for all of the prepositional phrases of the sentence, be sure to either include it only at the beginning of the first prepositional phrase or in front of each of the phrases. (In other words, if you only use the preposition at the start of two of three phrases, the sentence would not be parallel.)

Example: Waldo could be found everywhere—**in** the park, the grocery store, and the picket line.

or

Waldo could be found everywhere—**in** the park, **in** the grocery store, and **in** the picket line.

not

Waldo could be found everywhere—**in** the park, the grocery store, and **in** the picket line.

4. **Match infinitive phrases (*to* + verb) with infinitive phrases**

Note: Just like the example above with prepositional phrases, the word *to* must also be placed in front of the first infinitive phrase only or in front of all infinitive phrases.

Example: Deep Creek, Maryland provides a host of activities for the family **to** exercise, shop, and relax.

or

Deep Creek, Maryland provides a host of activities for the family **to** exercise, **to** shop, and **to** relax.

not

Deep Creek, Maryland provides a host of activities for the family **to** exercise, shop, and **to** relax.

5. **Match gerund (always ends in *-ing* and functions as a noun) phrases with gerund phrases**

Example: Scouring Pinterest, clipping coupons, and shopping sales keep me entertained for hours each weekend.

6. **Match participle (ends in either *-ing* or *-ed* and functions as an adjective) phrases with participle phrases**

Example: Because she believed in the mission of teaching, Candy braced herself for the start of another year of arguing kids, blinding migraines, and grueling hours.

7. **When designing elements in a list, make sure that each bulleted or enumerated item is written in the same grammatical format.**

   Example: The five design elements of a document include:

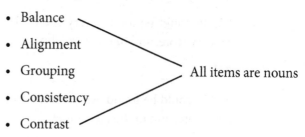

- Balance
- Alignment
- Grouping
- Consistency
- Contrast

All items are nouns

PRACTICE EXERCISE 2.5

Directions: Correct any parallelism errors. Write C beside any correct sentence.

1. As the siren blared, I tried to determine if I should stop, pull over, or should I just keep driving?

2. The babysitter remembered to bathe the children, to read a bedtime story, and turn on the nightlight in their bedroom.

3. Amy was enamored with her husband's vocal talent, sense of humor, and that he loved adventure.

4. Susie and Stacy frequently shared rides to their small group because they enjoyed talking, laughing, and singing together in the car.

5. Throughout their marriage, Ron never failed to present his wife with a card on Valentine's Day, their anniversary, on her birthday, Easter, and on Christmas.

MODIFIER ERRORS

Modifiers are words that change (or modify) the meaning of another word by adding detail or description.

Modifier errors are some of the funniest grammatical errors you can find, but in the spirit of being grammatically correct, they must be corrected...sigh.

1. **Dangling modifiers: The verbal phrase at the beginning of a sentence describes the subject of the sentence. Dangling modifiers occur when the verbal phrase does not correctly describe the subject.**

    Dangling modifier   subject

    Incorrect: Failing to navigate the hairpin turns, the treacherous path claimed the lives of two inexperienced bikers. (paths can't navigate turns...)

    To fix dangling modifiers, make sure the verbal phrase correctly describes the subject.

    Added the missing subject of the clause

    Correct: Because the bikers failed to navigate the hairpin turns, the treacherous path claimed the lives of two inexperienced bikers.

2. **Misplaced modifiers: Where you position the modifier affects the meaning of the sentence. Place the modifier (words, phrases, clauses) as close to the word you intend for it to describe.**

    Incorrect: The student had learned to never accept open containers of alcohol from his parents. (Ummmmm, if you can't trust your parents, then who CAN you trust?)

    modifier

    Correct: The student had learned from his parents to never accept open containers of alcohol. (Ahhhh, now THAT makes better sense!)

3. Limiting modifiers (words like *only, hardly, just, even,* and *almost*): Place these words directly before the word they describe. Again, their placement alters the meaning of the sentence.

   Example: *Just* I ate today. (means that no one else ate today, just me)

   Example: I *just* ate today. (means that I did nothing else today, just ate—not a very productive day)

   Example: I ate *just* today. (means that today was the only day I ate; I must be famished!)

4. Squinting modifiers: This occurs when a modifier is placed between two words in a sentence and the reader is unclear which word it is intended to describe; it can describe both. To fix this error, change the order of the sentence so that it is clear.

   Incorrect: Students who do not revise their papers *markedly* receive poor grades in my course. (Which is it? Does *markedly* refer to how much their papers are revised or to how low of a grade they receive?)

   Correct: Students who do not *markedly* revise their papers receive poor grades in my course.

   Correct: Students who do not revise their papers receive *markedly* poor grades in my course.

PRACTICE EXERCISE 2.6

Directions: Correct the modifier error in each of these sentences.

1. Carla misses frequently getting together with her former college roommates.

2. Reading the stories of attempted child abductions in the neighborhood, the baby was never out of her mother's sight.

3. Evelyn retrieved her donkey in her pink floral housecoat.

4. Bart only said it would cost $20 for the shuttle to the airport.

5. The dog scared the postal worker with its menacing growl.

Punctuation

part **3**

COMMA

1. **Before coordinating conjunction (FANBOYS: For, And, Nor, But, Or, Yet, So)**

   Remember that there needs to be a complete sentence on both sides of the conjunction. If the two parts that you are joining with a conjunction share the same subject, do not use a comma to separate them.

   The comma goes **before** the conjunction.

   Complete thought   Complete thought

   Correct: Harriet's legs felt like cement blocks, and she refused to move another step.

   Compound verb phrase

   Incorrect: Harriet's legs felt like cement blocks and refused to move another step.

   (No comma is necessary since both verb phrases share the same subject, *Harriet's legs.*)

2. **Between words, phrases, or clauses in a series**

   Example of words: Please be sure to pack things to occupy yourself for the long car ride, such as your iPad, snacks, and water bottles.

   Example of phrases: Meticulous about not leaving his scent, the hunter placed his clothes overnight in a garbage bag filled with leaves, showered with scent-eliminating soap, and doused himself with doe urine.

   Example of clauses: Mikayla fed the cats, Noah fed the dogs, and Brian packed the truck.

3. **Between coordinate adjectives not joined by *and* that describe the same noun**

   If you are unsure whether two adjectives are coordinate adjectives, subject them to these two tests:

   Test 1: Comma can be replaced by the word *and*.

   > **Needs a comma**: light, fluffy dessert (makes sense to say light *and* fluffy dessert)

   > **Does NOT need a comma:** dark chocolate candy (does **not** make sense to say dark *and* chocolate candy)

   Test 2: The order of adjectives can be reversed

   > **Needs a comma:** light, fluffy dessert (makes sense to say fluffy *and* light dessert)

   > **Does NOT need a comma:** dark chocolate candy (does **not** make sense to say chocolate *and* dark candy)

   For the visual learner, sometimes it helps to draw arrows to what the adjectives describe. If both adjectives describe the same noun, use a comma to separate them.

Needs a comma: light, fluffy dessert (Both light *and* fluffy describe dessert)

Does NOT need a comma: dark chocolate candy (*dark* describes chocolate; *chocolate* describes candy)

4. **After introductory phrase or clause—optional for short phrases or clauses that cannot be misread**

    - This is not optional for phrases or clauses of **four or more words.**

    Example phrase: Without so much as a backward glance to mom, the kindergartener bounded joyfully up the bus steps.

    Example clause: When the doors to the bus burst open, the kindergartener bounded joyfully up the bus steps.

5. **To set off nonessential elements**

    Nonessential information adds a bit more description to an element of the sentence, but is not essential to the meaning of the sentence. This information could be eliminated without dramatically changing the meaning of the sentence.

    - *That* never introduces a nonessential clause; therefore do not set *that* phrases or clauses off with commas.

    Example: The reticent child, shy by nature, clung firmly to her mother's leg.

6. **Interrupters such as modifiers, parenthetical expressions, and conjunctive adverbs**

These interrupt the flow of the sentence or digress.

a. **Modifiers:** on the other hand   for example   in fact
               in the first place   I believe   in my opinion
               fortunately   certainly

Example: Anomia, in my opinion, is a ridiculously fun card game, despite the extreme stress it induces.

b. **Conjunctive adverbs:** accordingly   anyhow   besides
                     consequently furthermore hence
                     however   indeed   instead
                     likewise   meanwhile   moreover
                     nevertheless otherwise   still
                     then   therefore   thus

Notice the difference in punctuation:

Example with semicolon and comma: The auditor found the error in the figures; **however,** the books still did not balance. (*However* separates two complete sentences.)

Example with two commas: The auditor found the error in the figures; the books, **however,** still did not balance. (*However* simply interrupts the flow of the sentence.)

c. **Parenthetical expressions**

Example: The wedding, as it turns out, was at 4:30 p.m. on Sunday instead of 1:00 as I had originally thought.

7. **Degrees, titles, and elements in dates, places, and addresses**

Example of degree: Kristin Oberg, M.A., engages students by making English fun to learn.

Example of title: Martin Luther King, Jr., believed in the equality of all men and fought tirelessly for Civil Rights.

Example of dates: On Monday, May 30, 2016, we celebrated Noah's 12th birthday.

Example of address: We depart for Bethesda, Maryland, tomorrow for a teaching conference.

8. **Contrast or emphasis and with tag questions**

   Example of tag question: Surely, you're not going to wear THAT shirt, are you?

   Example of contrast: When I saw the rat in my hallway, I intended to extract Brian, not Tim from the room.

9. **Mild interjections and yes/no**

   Example of a mild interjection: Well, I suppose the Ogdens won't be eating at that place again!

   Example of yes/no: No, their experience at the restaurant was awful, but the story they relayed about their experience was quite amusing.

10. **Direct address and after salutation of a personal letter**

    Example of direct address: "Bye, Felicia!"

    Example of personal salutation: Dear Liz,

11. **Quoted matter**

    Example: "Yes, Barry White," Kari stuttered in embarrassment, "I would love to do your morning announcements."

12. **Prevent misreading or mark an omission**

    Confusing: Although I should have studied harder. (seems like a fragment)

    Clearer: Although, I should have studied harder.

    Example of marking an omission: To err is human; to forgive, divine. (verb *is* omitted)

PRACTICE EXERCISE 3.1

Directions: Insert commas where appropriate. Write C by any correct sentence.

1. Uncle Ken when are you coming to visit me?

2. Painting the picnic shelter cleaning the shower rooms and vacuuming the pool all need to be completed before Saturday's reunion.

3. Noah the one with a great sense of humor always seemed to have a witty response for everything.

4. Paul constructed a heavy-duty wagon to use with his quad and built a porch swing as a gift for his wife.

5. The energetic fidgety child accidentally spilled her red Kool Aid on her mother's tan plaid jacket.

6. Since they had only traveled about thirty minutes of their four-hour trip the father ignored the child's pleas for a potty break.

QUOTATION MARKS

Use quotation marks to enclose a speaker's exact words.

1. **Use a comma to introduce the quotation. Capitalize the first word of a complete sentence inside a quotation, and always place a comma or period INSIDE the closing quotation marks.**

   Example: Kari said, "This house looks like the dorm room of a freshman about to flunk out for partying too much! Throw that mac and cheese bowl AWAY and get that bottle of Naked juice outta [sic] the living room NOW!"

2. **In a single quoted sentence that is interrupted by *he said* or *she said*, do not capitalize the first word in the second part of the sentence.**

   Example: "Who knew you could get electrocuted," Kari exclaimed, "in your ears and jaw from headphones and a scarf full of static electricity?"

3. **If there are two quoted sentences interrupted by *he said* or *she said*, do capitalize the first word of the second sentence. Also notice that the period comes after the *he said* or *she said*.**

   Example: "I just burned my leg with hot icing that dropped off of a cinnamon roll," Kari said. "Life coach needed; apply today."

4. **Use quotation marks to enclose single words for emphasis.**

   Example: Click now to complete our survey for a "free" iPhone.

5. **Use a comma for titles of articles, poems, stories, songs, and speeches. (No comma is needed before the quotation marks in these examples.)**

   Example: "Rose for Miss Emily" recounts a chilling tale of unrequited love.

6. Use single quotation marks to enclose a quotation within a quotation.

Example: Bennett Brauer, newscaster on *SNL*, said, "Well, maybe I don't 'look the part.' I'm not 'svelte.' I don't 'get along with people' when I go to work...."

Quotation Marks and Punctuation

1. Periods and commas ALWAYS go *inside* quotation marks.

Example: "Please hurry," the bus driver urged.

2. Colons and semicolons ALWAYS go *outside* quotation marks.

Example: The instructor reminded the students, "If I see your cell phone out during a test, you will receive a failing grade"; Zach found out the hard way that she was serious.

3. A question mark or an exclamation point goes *inside* if the quoted material itself requires a question mark or an exclamation point. (It also goes *inside* if BOTH the entire sentence and the quoted material are a question or an exclamation.)

Example: "Did I say you could get down from that chair?" the mother asked.

4. A question mark or an exclamation point goes *outside* if the quoted material itself is not a question or an exclamation.

Example: Did the instructor really say, "Peace out, y'all"?

ITALICS

1. Titles of books, magazines, newspapers, movies, plays, and television shows

Example: Every married couple would benefit from seeing the powerful movie, *War Room*.

2. Names of works of art and the names of ships, trains, and planes

Example: Gilligan and his friends probably steer clear of boats after their experience on the *S.S. Minnow*.

PRACTICE EXERCISE 3.2

Directions: Insert quotation marks (double or single) and italics as needed. Punctuate and capitalize words correctly.

1. Look at the baby deer Sandy remarked as she strolled through the thick forest.

2. Just send a car, please Kari shouted into the phone breathlessly I'm on a pink bike with a Slim Jim can strapped to it with a bungee cord.

3. Heather stood proudly beside her recent purchase: her new car with 38,000 miles on it.

4. English is my favorite subject Jonathan sarcastically responded as he received his graded writing assignment.

5. Priscilla Shirer's newest book Fervent both challenged me and made me laugh.

APOSTROPHE

You are not alone if you still don't know when to use *its* vs. *it's*. Allow me, please, to try to simplify things for you.

Apostrophes have **two primary uses:**

1. **Possession: When you want to show ownership, you add an apostrophe.**

   - Add *'s* for possessive of nouns not ending in *s*. (Tyler's letter)
   - Add the apostrophe and *s* to the last word in a hyphenated noun (brother-in-law's car)
   - Do **not** use apostrophe to show the plural of proper nouns. (The MacQuarries will be joining us.)
   - Use *'* only (no *s*) to form the possessive of **plural** nouns ending in *s*. (boys' clubhouse)
   - Do **not** use an apostrophe with personal pronouns like *his, hers, theirs, its, ours*. (They are already possessive.)
   - Use *'s* with only the last noun for joint possession in a pair or series. (Kathy and Dan's home)

   Exceptions: Use an apostrophe to form the plural of

   - Acronyms (Dr. Olsen reminded her students to complete the SRTE's.)
   - Words being named (Please circle all of the is's and was's in your essay.)
   - Lowercase letters (How many i's does the sign contain?)

2. **Omission: Use an apostrophe for omitted numbers and letters.**

   Example: As the running back for the opposing team marches down the field with ease, my husband screams, "Get 'em!"

The plurals for numerals, letters, and years may be written with or without apostrophes, as long as no confusion results, and you are consistent.

PRACTICE EXERCISE 3.3

Directions: Underline the correct word choice in each sentence.

1. The teacher labeled the children's/childrens' supplies and stored them in cubbies.

2. Susan looks forward to spending time with the Millers/Miller's at Family Camp.

3. Its/It's best to provide a wide girth around a goose with its/it's goslings.

4. Jasons/Jason's plan required scissors/scissor's and duct tape.

5. He also needed to borrow his mother's-in-law/mother-in-law's hairdryer.

6. When seeing their owner approach with food in hand, the dog's/dogs' barking grew increasingly louder.

HYPHEN

1. **Two or more words acting as a single modifier before a noun**

   Example: The well-dressed executive assistant spilled his coffee down the front of his designer shirt. (It is not the *well* executive assistant as opposed to the sick one, and it is not the *dressed* executive assistant as opposed to the naked one. *Well* and *dressed* are acting as a single descriptor.)

   Exceptions:

   - When the first word of the modifier is an adverb ending in *-ly* (freshly fallen snow)
   - When modifier comes after a noun

   Example: The executive assistant was well dressed.

2. **Compound numbers from twenty-one through ninety-nine**

3. **Prefixes *ex-* (meaning former), *self-*, *all-***

   Example: The ex-tenant sued his landlord for keeping his security deposit.

4. **Suffix *-elect***

   Example: President-elect

5. **Between a prefix and a capitalized word**

   Example: mid-January

6. **To avoid confusion or an awkward combination of letters**

   Example: re-sign the contract vs. resign from a job

PRACTICE EXERCISE: 3.4

Directions: Add hyphens where necessary. Write C beside any correct sentence.

1. The thirty five year old executive still lived rent free in his parent's home.

2. The "Chewbacca mom" turned into one of the most watched videos on social media overnight.

3. Struggling to climb the stairs, it was evident to the veterinarian that Bojangles was well fed.

4. Stepping into Subway, the smell of freshly baked bread awakens your olfactory system.

5. The prudent buyer purchased the less expensive model.

CPSIA information can be obtained
at www.ICGtesting.com
Printed in the USA
LVOW05s1652231217
559490LV00007B/16/P